J.E.Mitchell

Grindstones and Grindstone Fixtures

J.E.Mitchell

Grindstones and Grindstone Fixtures

ISBN/EAN: 9783337321369

Printed in Europe, USA, Canada, Australia, Japan

Cover: Foto ©Thomas Meinert / pixelio.de

More available books at **www.hansebooks.com**

A Grindstone of the 16th Century.

PRINTED BY H. SCHOPPERUM, FRANKFORT-ON-MAIN, IN 1548.

THE GRINDSTONE.

ITS ANTIQUITY.

In the whole range of mechanics, with all modern developments and enlarged capabilities, there has been applied no mechanism nor process yet able to supersede the grindstone in its peculiar office. It is the one thing in mechanic arts that improvement has not added to, or invention displaced; while the pruning hook and plough are of equal antiquity, the spirit of improvement has touched both but left the grindstone unchanged. Its utility in the early ages was great, and science has not lessened its value any by its perfection of other means for like results. It has been found in use among uncivilized people, and yet has its place with nations most advanced. Writers of fiction knew it would not conflict with the appearance of truth to ascribe it a place among barbarians. It is among the few implements of handicraft mentioned in Scripture, though there only named for milling purposes; it is the same in form and in universal use—a round revolving stone. In a scriptural research for the articles of handicraft mentioned then, we can look through the "eye of a needle" and find the grindstone beyond, its origin lost in the darkness of antiquity. It is not meant to confound the mill stone of antiquity with the grindstone of to-day, which the Encyclopedia mentions as "a flattish circular stone of various diameters, employed in the cutting and sharpening of edged tools, precious stones, &c., and the grinding of steel, glass, pottery and the like.

They are made of sandstone, or sandstone grit." The grindstone now has scarcely a wider capability or greater usefulness that when we first hear of it. Although .limited as its qualifications may be, it serves its purpose as nothing else can. Improvement has furnished us wheels of composition which only to some extent serve some of its purposes, but the grindstone still remains unsupplanted. It is a tool of the utmost nicety in proper hands and properly understood, and is capable of performing with speed and precision its limited agency, beyond the powers of any modern tool. It is perhaps found best handled in its purpose of grinding dies for cut nails, where its proper use constitutes an occupation not to be attained very perfectly by a short apprenticeship with it. That known as the "bead stone," used by makers of cut nails, is a tool of the utmost perfection of workmanship, not to be meddled with by the inexperienced, however lightly, without the result being noticed by the eye of the experienced nailer. The milling machine, the planer, the file, the lathe and emery wheel, do much of the work of the grindstone, but it still performs to perfection its needful though limited purposes. The importance and nicety of it, as a means to a purpose, is only known by those who know how to prepare and keep it in order.

Its utility or importance could not be guessed at, were one to look at a crooked and badly kept grindstone; but in the hands of those who know its merit, with its even surface running as true as any turned wheel, it will perform work with a rapidity and precision attainable by no other means. In the hands of those who are learned in its use and keeping, it is capable of adaptation to intricate and fine work, but with those who do not understand it, it is rude, and the very opposite of what the educated craftsman would select for any purpose of fine employment.

An heirloom of antiquity, but used among us as we received it, and without any attachment or improvement; capable of its complete functions only when well kept and well applied, and this is only found with those whose craft-education is solely to handle it. It alone can cut and shape expeditiously that which is prepared to cut and shape all other hard materials—cast steel hardened. It is still employed to give the finest edge, the most even surface, the brightest polish, and is the quickest to accomplish it. The emery wheel does but a few of its purposes, and nothing that we have could supply its place. The file has its own peculiar uses, but in contact with the grindstone, its thousand small cutting edges would be reduced to polished plainness. It is found a necessary implement on the farm, and is still required where the finest of instruments are made, or the hardest of metals are worked. It has come to us as we have it, and in all likelihood will pass on down to other ages the same—a simple circular stone, swiftly revolving on an axle.

It accompanies those who " go down to the sea in great ships," and moves along the frontier with the advance of civilization. All nations use it, and it is perhaps, with all, the one piece of mechanism that bears the same form, and is the same in principle. More or less directly it takes part in the greatest modern material enterprises; it has, no doubt, assisted to fashion the implements of many of the lost arts, and is still needed in many of the requirements of arts of the present day.

As ages revolve and invention gives to the world new devices, may it be found more the agent in forming the ploughshare and pruning hook, than in sharpening the sword.—*Lewis's Pamphlet, No. 9.*

6

GRINDSTONES.

THE OLDEST ESTABLISHMENT IN THIS COUNTRY.

ABOUT the year 1769, a few tons of grindstones arrived in Philadelphia from Newcastle on Tyne, England, consigned to Joshua Fisher & Sons. This old-fashioned Quaker firm were located on Dock street, below Second, and kept their stock of grindstones chained together on the sidewalk to prevent larceny. From this small beginning Philadelphia has become the headquarters for the manufacture and sale of grindstones in this country.

About the year 1810, James Mitchell started the business in Philadelphia at the junction of Fourth street and the old York Road, so called because it was the old post road to New York, when the mail was carried in stages through in two days by the "fast line." The buildings erected at that time are still in existence and occupied by J. E. Mitchell, the son and successor of James Mitchell, who died in 1851. Since that time these buildings have been largely increased in size, and a large factory erected on Beach street, above Green, in which the manufacture of grindstones and grindstone fixtures is carried on extensively by the aid of steam power and large lathes, on which the stones are turned off perfectly true and ready for use by means of improved tools and patented machinery. A grindstone of 5,000 pounds can be adjusted on the shaft and made perfectly true in a short time; in this way our machinists avoid the delay and dust of finishing them in their own shops. By means of a patent machine for the manufacture of small grindstones they are made with great speed and perfection and at a small cost. Gangs of saws are attached to the steam power by means of which the broken and damaged grindstones are sawed into slabs of various thicknesses, which are placed in a cutting machine which makes them into grindstones at the rate of seven in ten minutes. These are used by cutlers for grinding table knives, razors, etc. A harder stone is imported from Europe in blocks, which are also sawed in slabs of one inch thick and made into the famous Craigleith wheels, the only article yet discovered which will cut glass. All the beautiful cut work on wine glasses, decanters, globes, and the delicate tracery and landscapes on the plate glass vestibule doors are all done with this stone, which is so hard that it can only be dressed with flint stone or diamond.

GRINDSTONES.

WHERE THEY COME FROM AND HOW THEY ARE MADE.

THE sandstone formation overlying the coal beds of England, furnishes the grindstones of that country, the principal quarries being located at New Castle on Tyne and at Wickersly. The quarries are worked by hand, and all the grindstones are made with mallet and chisel, and have been imported into this country for over one hundred years. The grindstones from the provinces of Nova Scotia and New Brunswick are, also, the overlying sandstone formation of the coal district bordering on the Bay of Fundy and extending across the province to the Gulf of St. Lawrence. These immense deposits contain a great variety of grits known as Nova Scotia grindstones. These quarries are generally worked by the French people, known as Acadians, from the name they gave this country, "Acadia," and are the descendants of the Huguenots, who were driven out of France by religious persecution. They are a very industrious and simple-minded people, and the females retain to this day the style of dress brought over from France by their ancestors. The tides of the Bay of Fundy rise and fall from 60 to 70 feet every twelve hours, and these people avail themselves of this power to work the quarries, which extend from a high bluff on the mainland down to low water mark in the bay. At low water a huge mass of stone is loosened from its bed and a heavy chain is passed under it and over a large boat which is placed alongside. As the tide rises the stone attached to the bottom of the boat is floated into a sand cove at high water, and made into a grindstone after the tide recedes. This is done with mallet and chisel, the rough parts being first chopped off with a heavy axe. Machinery has been recently introduced, and the small grindstones are now turned in a lathe by steam power. The sandstone deposits of this country which are made into grindstones, are found along the shores of Lake Erie and extending for a considerable distance east and west of Cleveland, and inland as far as Marietta, on the Ohio. They are also found on the shores of Lake Huron, above Detroit. These deposits are of a different character from the foreign stone and do not seem to be the overlying strata of coal formations, but appear to be a later formation as the quarries look as though this part of Ohio had once been the bottom of the lake, the sand of which had become solid and been up-heaved by some convulsion of nature. Nearly all the Ohio grindstones are made by machinery driven by steam power.

The blocks of stone being loosened from the quarry bed are roughly hewn out with a square hole in the centre, they are then placed on a heavy square iron shaft furnished with a nine inch collar, against which the stone is securely fastened by means of another collar keyed against the stone. The shaft and stone being driven by steam power, two men on opposite sides of the stone turn it off perfectly true by means of soft iron bars six feet long, two inches by one-half inch thick, which are drawn out to a thin point which is curved upward. This was formerly a very unhealthy operation, owing to the dust being inhaled by the workmen, but this difficulty is now obviated by means of blowers which drive it away.

THE GRINDSTONE.

ITS USES.

THERE are specialties in mechanic arts which are the results of many years of practice, and in nothing more than in the varied and important uses to which grindstones are applied. Formerly their operations were confined to the sharpening of tools only, but this is now only a small part of the uses to which they are put, as it has been found by experience that almost every kind of steel, iron and brass work used in finished machines can be ground better and cheaper than by filing. Almost every part of a locomotive engine is now finished on the grindstone, which leaves the metal in the best possible condition to receive the polish or paint in finishing. The Baldwin Works, Philadelphia, keep six grindstones of 4000 pounds each running constantly on locomotive work alone, not only all the rough castings being ground, but forty-one working parts of the engine are finished in this way, besides grinding off the faces of their anvils, some of them weighing 700 pounds. The master machinists of nearly all the railway repair shops find it to their interest to keep at least one grindstone in use for this purpose.

Grindstones are also used for finishing pulleys of all sizes. The pulley is caused to revolve against the stone, which runs rapidly in an opposite direction, this grinds down the face of the pulley very fast, and at less cost than turning it off in a lathe, besides leaving it perfectly true. It requires, however, a very peculiar grindstone for this purpose, the grit of which should be very sharp and firm, so as not to crush down with the necessary pressure, and yet not so hard as to glaze in using. A peculiar kind of New Castle grindstone has been found to meet these requirements, and should be used with water to prevent heating.

MACHINISTS' GRINDSTONES.

THERE is probably no implement in the machine shop or factory which pays better for the care bestowed on it than the grindstone, and when we consider that nearly every tool and all edge tools require its use, it is somewhat surprising that more attention has not been bestowed on the proper selection of the grit for the purposes intended. The writer has frequently observed in many machine shops that a good grindstone well hung and in perfect order was the exception rather than the rule. As grindstones in such places are almost constantly in use, their first cost is of little consequence if the quality is calculated to do the work required in the shortest time and most perfect manner, as more time can be wasted on a poor grindstone, badly hung and out of order, than will pay for a good one every three months. This state of things should not continue, as with the great improvements made in the manner of hanging them, and the endless variety of grits to select from, every machinist and manufacturer should have a grindstone which will not only do its work perfectly, but in the shortest time. This can be accomplished by sending a small sample of the grit wanted to the dealer to select by. Grindstones are frequently injured through the carelessness of those having them in charge. The machinist's grindstone will have a soft place in it caused by a part of it being allowed to stand in water over night and the difficulty arising from this cause increases with every revolution of the stone; but as this homely implement is in charge of all the men in the shop in general, and no one in particular, and as all the workmen are too busy to raze it down, double the time is consumed in imperfectly grinding a tool, than would be required to grind it perfectly if the stone was kept in order by some one whose duty it should be to attend to keeping all the grindstones of the establishment in order. The wages of a man for this duty would be saved in the time and perfection with which the tools of a large establishment could be kept in order for work.

HINTS HOW TO USE A GRINDSTONE.

1st.—Don't waste the stone by running it in water, nor allow it to stand in water when not in use, as this will cause a soft place.

2d.— Wet the stone by dropping water on it from a pot suspended above the stone, and stop off the water when not in use.

3d.—Don't allow the stone to get out of order, but keep it perfectly round by the use of a piece of gas pipe or a hacker, or use a pair of the double hung stones, which keep each other in order.

4th.—Clean off all greasy tools before sharpening, as grease or oil destroys the grit.

5th.— Observe— When you get a stone that suits your purpose, send a sample of the grit to the dealer to select by; a half ounce sample is enough, and can be sent in a letter by mail.

FARMERS' GRINDSTONES.

THERE is no implement so essential, and no one to which so little attention is paid as the grindstone.. The worn out and worse than worthless " hubbs " of the neighboring saw or edge tool factory, with a wooden axle, and set in the crotch of a tree, is considered, by some who know no better, as being all that is necessary to a farm in all other respects, perhaps, well stocked. But with the introduction of greatly improved agricultural implements, mowing machines especially, the need has been felt for something better than these primitive arrangements, and in order to keep pace with this onward march, improvements have been introduced, both in the grit and manufacture, as well as in the mode of hanging this indispensable article which, perhaps, may be new to most person.

The best grindstones are now made by machinery which renders them mathematically true, and the grit being selected of only the best quality, the getting of a good one is reduced almost to a certainty. The ordinary square cranks have been superseded by those made on the self adjusting principles which consists of a round shaft on which a screw is cut, and two plates, which are screwed together with a burr, so as to suit any thickness of stone which, by pressing against the sides of the stone instead of the shaft being wedged into the eye, prevents any possibility of splitting the stone, while at the same time it causes it to hang perfectly true on the crank. Another mprovement is in the use of friction rollers, thereby reducing the friction just one-half and enabling the farmer, with the use of a treadle, to grind any small tool without calling off some one from his work to " turn the grindstone." No grindstone should be exposed to the weather, as it not only injures the wood work, but the sun's rays harden the stone so much in time, as to render it useless; neither should it be run in water, as the part remaining in water softens so much that it wears away faster than the other side, and many a " soft place " in a stone has arisen from this cause alone and not from any inequality in the grit. The proper way is to allow the water to drop on the stone as it is needed, from an iron water cup, or, what answers very well, an old white lead keg, supported above the stone, with a spile near the bottom which can be driven in when not needed, and if kept filled with water will last a long time. Finally the stone should not be allowed to get " out of rouud," as no tool can be properly ground unless the stone runs true. If it should become uneven get some one to turn it, and with a nail rod raze it down until it becomes perfectly round. Greasy or rusty tools should be well cleaned before grinding, or they will choke up the grit. If this should occur, a board pressed against the stone and a little sharp sand dropped between it and the stone while the latter is turning, will clean it off and sharpen up the grit.

GRINDSTONES.

HOW TO HANG AND USE THEM.

THERE is probably no appliance of the machine shop, or manufactory, to which so little attention is paid as to the grindstone, and it is very rare indeed, that this useful tool is found to be in perfect order. This is the more remarkable considering the great improvements made in the manufacture of iron and steel tools, on the perfection of which the precision and proper grit of the grindstone has a very important bearing. We propose to try to remedy this omission by offering some suggestions as to the selecttion of suitable grits, and the proper mode of adjusting, using and keeping grindstones in order.

There have been very decided improvements made over the old style of fixtures for hanging grindstones, which generally consisted of a square shaft, which was wedged into a square hole in the middle of the stone, at the imminent risk of bursting the stone when at rest, or of endangering the life of the grinder when in motion. Now, all shafts, from the smallest to the largest, are made of round iron (wrought,) with a screw and nut, by means of which two cast iron plates are pressed against the sides of the stone, which is firmly held by pressure and friction, and relieving it from any tendency to burst, and adjusting it with the greatest precision. These plates are sometimes bolted to the sides of the stone, with a square shaft on which the stone is adjusted by means of screws passing through a projecting rim on the plates, but we think these holes have a tendency to weaken the stone.

Before adjusting the stone on the shaft the two sides should be made perfectly parallel, so that the flanges will bear evenly; then adjust the shaft, and if the stone does not run true the high side can be placed uppermost, and by gently unscrewing the nut and striking the stone it can be made to drop the desired distance, which can be indicated by the flange. In our largest establishments the stones are turned off perfectly true outside of the shop, so as to avoid the dust which injures the machinery, and by leaving a depression in the sides of the stone of the size of the flange it will run true without further labor. After being thus adjusted it should be kept true by the free use of the hacker, and should not be allowed to stand in water. A diamond carbon tool is used where great nicety is required, and the sides of the stone are painted, (without the use of oil, however,) in order to prevent the moisture from entering, and thereby keeping the edges square.

The following article from the Technologist, gives a good idea of the process of sharpening tools. Edge tools are fitted up by grinding, very much as a plank would be reduced in thickness were a large plane employed in which were set a hundred or more very small gouges, each cutting a narrow grove. The sharp grit of the grindstone being harder than the iron or steel, cuts very small channels in the surface of the metal, and the revolving disc carries away all the minute particles that are detached by the grit. If we were to examine the surface of a tool that has just been removed from a grindstone, under the lens of a powerful microscope, it would appear as it were like the rough surface of a field which has been recently scarified with some implement which formed alternate ridges and furrows. Hence, as these ridges and furrows run together from both sides at the cutting edge, the newly ground edge seems to be formed of a system of minute teeth rather than to consist of a smooth edge. For this reason a tool is first ground on a coarse stone, so as to wear the surface of the steel away rapidly. Then it is polished on a wheel of much finer grit, and finally, in order to reduce the serrature as much as possible, a whetstone of the finest grit must be employed. This gives a cutting edge having the smallest possible serration. A razor, for example, does not have a perfect cutting edge, as one may perceive by viewing it through a microscope, and yet the serrations are actually so much smaller than a human hair that the minute teeth cut the hair in twain, but when the serrations on the edge of the razor become so battered up and dull that they will not sever a hair or cut a man's beard off, the edge must be honed and strapped until the system of minute teeth will be so much smaller than a hair that several of them will take hold of the smallest hair at once. These suggestions will furnish something of an idea of the operation in grinding and whetting edge tools. Beginners are sometimes instructed, when grinding edge tools, to have the stone revolve toward the cutting edge, and sometimes from it. When the first grinding is being done, this is a matter of indifference, but when the finishing touches are applied near and at the very edge, a grinder can always complete his task with more accuracy if the periphery of the grindstone revolves towards the cutting edge, as the steel that is worn away will be removed more easily. Whereas, when a stone runs in the opposite direction, the grinder cannot always tell exactly when the side of the tool is fully ground up to the edge. This is more especially true when the steel has a rather low or soft temper. The stone, when running away from the edge, will not sweep away every particle of the metal that hangs as a " feather," but when the stone revolves towards the edge, there will be no " feather edge " to deceive the eye of the grinder.

WHY DO GRINDSTONES BURST?

In olden times, grindstones were always made with a square hole in the centre, about six inches across, in which a square iron shaft was placed, and the stone adjusted by means of wooden wedges, driven around the shaft with sufficient force to hold the stone securely in its place, and to resist the power applied to the shaft when dressing the stone off. This resistance at the edge, being equal to a lever purchase of half the diameter of the stone, has a tendency to burst the stone by the pressure of the shaft in the eye of the stone, which is also frequently augmented by the swelling of the wood employed as wedges.

Bursting of grindstones was a common occurrence under these circumstances, happening sometimes soon after the stone was hung, but frequently after being weakened by wearing away a part of it. Grindstones are generally hung at nail works by means of two heavy cast iron plates with square holes and a heavy square boss cast on the outside. Four holes are bored through the stones near the corners of the eye, corresponding with the four similar holes in the plates, through which four bolts pass and fasten the plates securely to the sides of the stone by means of nuts. A square shaft passes through the centre of the plates, and the stone is adjusted by means of eight set screws passing through the boss, and resting against the sides of the square shaft. This relieves the eye of the stone from any strain, but the tendency of the four holes in lines with the corners of the eye is to weaken the stone in these directions. A case occurred of grindstones having been burst by using cast iron plates with a square boss four inches long, cast on the inside of the plates and tapering towards the end, which was fitted snug into the eye of the stone, and the plates being pressed against its sides, the tapering boss acted as a wedge, and two

2

stones were burst in this way before the cause was discovered.

The best mode of hanging a grindstone is on a round
shaft of wrought iron on which a collar is forged, with
two cast iron plates of about one-third the diameter of the
stone in size, and dished so as to bear on the outside edge
only. A screw is cut on the shaft and fitted with a heavy
nut, by means of which the two plates are pressed against
the sides of the stone, holding it firmly by pressure and
friction alone and relieving the eye from all strain. A
stone hung in this manner should not burst except by
centrifugal force, caused by the stone being run at a very
high rate of speed ; but stones do burst even when hung
so, and when not running at a dangerous rate of speed.
As the bursting of a grindstone is always fraught with
great danger to the workmen using it, and in its vicinity,
it becomes of considerable interest to know the cause.
Grindstones vary very much in their composition and in
the manner in which their particles are held together.
Some stones are composed of grains of pure sand, which
have been pressed together with little or no cementing
material, leaving numerous interstices among their particles. In others, the particles of sand are cemented
together with clay, rendering the stone much more compact and strong. A stone of the first kind, being porous,
will weigh less to the cubic foot than the latter, and will
absorb more water when in use, thereby rendering it still
less strong. The quantity of water absorbed by a stone
of this character has been proved by actual experiment to
be equal to 12 pounds to the cubic foot, while in the
closer and more compact stones it is but $5\frac{1}{2}$ pounds, so
that if a dry porous stone of 6 feet diameter by 12 inches
thick contains 27 cubic feet, it will absorb 324 pounds of
water when in use; and when such a stone is allowed to
stand over night, a considerable portion of the water will
settle in the lower half of the stone, while the upper being
exposed to a free circulation of air, will lose its water by

evaporation and will be left comparatively dry, so that no matter how true the stone may be dressed, the effect, when in motion, will be the same as of a badly balanced fly wheel, and with a little increase of the usual speed, the tendency will be, of the wet side, to fly off from the rest of the stone, or in other words, to burst the stone. A case of this kind recently occurred in New Jersey. A workman had been using a stone of this character for grinding sad irons. The stone being completely saturated with water over night, the following morning he started the stone, (which was about 6 feet diameter by 1 foot thick,) and after working a short time, had occasion to step aside for a few moments, when the stone burst, a portion of it passing through the roof and lodging in the side of an adjoining building, another struck a heavy driving shaft in front of the stone, and a third fell in the pit in which the stone was running. The usual speed of this stone was about 180 turns a minute, which it is supposed was somewhat increased by the absence of the grinder. The increase of the speed of an unequally balanced stone of a porous character caused it to burst. Great care should be exercised in examining a stone for defects before hanging it. This can be best done by washing off the sides and edge with water and a broom, and if any crack be discovered, the stone should be rejected. No part of a grindstone should be allowed to stand in water when not in use, as this would but increase the tendency to burst in the manner above referred to, besides causing a soft place.

TURNING TOOL

FOR TURNING OFF STONE, AND FOR

DRESSING GRINDSTONES.

Patented by J. E. MITCHELL, Philadelphia, April 9th, 1872.

MANNER of HOLDING the TOOL FOR TURNING OFF GRINDSTONES.

This Tool, consisting of a holder and one dozen cutters, is
manufactured and for sale only by the Patentee.

THE object of this tool is to turn off stones of any kind and to any required shape. Columns may be turned off perfectly true, and any form of mouldings may be given to Bases and Capitals, or to Balusters, Vases and other forms of ornamental work in stone. The stone is roughly rounded off and hung upon proper centres, and caused to revolve slowly. The tool is held on the rest at such an angle as to cut under the surface of the stone and reduce the same to the desired form by peeling off layers in small scales. The stone can then be finished with sand and water, and polished in the usual way. In this manner stones may be shaped much more readily than by the use of ordinary tools, which only exert a scraping action. This tool is especially adapted for turning and trueing grindstones in machine shops, as it makes little or no dust, and having used it very extensively for this purpose in our own business, we can recommend it with confidence.

The handsome column, containing forty varieties of grindstones, together with the entire display at the Centennial Exposition, were turned off with above tool.

GRINDSTONES.

THE VARIOUS KINDS IN USE.

THE *English*, *Nova Scotia* and *Ohio* grindstones are the principal kinds in use, but each of these sorts is subdivided into an endless variety of sizes and grits.

ENGLISH GRINDSTONES.

NEW CASTLE.—Yellow color and sharp grit; the fine soft ones for grinding saws, and the coarser and harder ones for sad irons and springs, pulleys and shafting, (instead of turning,) and for bead and face stones in nail works, and for castings, (dry grinding.)

WICKERSLY.—Grayish yellow color; for grinding saws, squares, bevels, and cutlers' work generally. A very soft grit to avoid taking out the temper.

LIVERPOOL, (or Melling.)—Of a red color and very sharp grit; for saws and edge tools generally. An excellent grit for sharpening axes in ship yards.

NOVA SCOTIA.—Blue or yellowish gray color, and of all grits, from the finest and hardest to the coarsest and softest; the large ones for grinding sad irons and hinges, springs and edge tools; the medium and small sizes for machine shops and for sharpening edge tools generally.

BAY CHALEUR, N. B.—Of a uniform blue color and soft, sharp grit; for manufacturing table cutlery, and is admirably adapted for machinists' tools, and for sharpening edge tools generally, when a fine edge is required.

OHIO.

BEREA.—White color, fine and sharp grit; for sharpening edge tools generally.

AMHERST, (Black River.)—Brownish white color, soft, loose grit; for edge tools, and the very soft ones for saws.

INDEPENDENCE.—Grayish white color, and coarse sharp grit; for grinding springs and files, and for dry grinding of castings.

MASSILLON.—Yellowish white color, coarse, sharp grit; for edge tools, springs, files, and nail cutters' face stones, and for dry grinding of castings.

HURON, (Michigan.)—Of a uniform blue color, and fine, sharp grit; good for sharpening tools when a very fine edge is required.

GLASS CUTTERS' GRINDSTONES,

of New Castle, Warrington, Craigleith, and Yorkshire grits; for checkering, mitering, fluting and for punty stones.

CUTLERS' GRINDSTONES,

of New Castle, Nova Scotia, and Wickersly grits; made to order, of any size.

Shank Stones; for table cutlery.

CURRIERS' RUBSTONES,

of New Castle, Nova Scotia, and Ohio grits; for first and second stones; and Scotch Water of Ayr, Welsh, and Hindostan, for clearing stones.

SCYTHE, OIL AND WHET STONES,

Ouachita, Arkansas, Orange, and Scotch Water of Ayr stones and hones, of all shapes. Shoemakers' rubbers, and scythestones of all sizes.

GRINDSTONES, MADE BY PATENTED MACHINERY.

These are made of suitable grit for sharpening Machinists' and Planing Mill tools and for Cutlers', Glass-cutters' and Dentists' use. They are perfectly round, with the hole exactly in the centre, and of any required diameter and thickness. We also furnish shafts—for lathe use—on which several stones of different sizes can be used at the same time.

MACHINISTS' IMPROVED

DOUBLE HUNG GRINDSTONES, No. 1.

THE accompanying cut represents a mode of hanging grindstones which is very popular in England, although not used to any extent in this country. Its advantages over the old method consists in having two grindstones, a coarse and fine one if desired, hung in one box, each stone having an independent motion, both lengthwise and lateral, by means of which they can be brought into contact when running at unequal rates of speed, and thereby keeping each other perfectly true, the lateral motion preventing the stones from cutting into rings. Grindstones hung in this manner, must, of necessity, remain perfectly round and straight on the face, thereby allowing the tool to be ground with the greatest precision, an absolute necessity in the present perfection of machinery. A tool of this kind in constant use soon overcomes its first cost by the time saved and the perfect work done, and it being made in the most durable manner, the machinery will outlast several sets of grindstones.

MACHINISTS' GRINDSTONES,
A SPECIALTY, No. 2.

See article on Machinists' Grindstones.

THE above cut represents a grindstone with iron fixtures, designed expressly for use in Railway Repair Shops, and for Machinists' use generally. They are light, durable and well made. The grindstone is turned off perfectly true and will be furnished of any desired grit—" New Castle " being the best for Machinists' tools, and " Bay Chaleur " for tools requiring a fine edge. For quality of stones furnished we refer to the Master Machinists of the various Railway Repair Shops, and Machinists generally, of this city.

SIZES.

PULLEYS EXTRA

30 by 4 inch stone and fixtures . . . . .
36 by 4 inch   "   "   "   . . . . .
48 by 6 inch   "   "   "   . . . . .
54 by 6 inch   "   "   "   . . . . .

Boxes furnished without stones if required.

N. B.—New Castle Stones, from 5 to 6½ feet diameter, of extra sharp grit, for grinding off wrought and cast iron work of Locomotives, and extensively used at the Baldwin Works. They are turned off perfectly true and fitted to the shafts.

FACTORY AND MACHINE SHOP, }   J. H. MITCHELL,
Nos. 602, 604 & 606 Beach St. }   *Superintendent.*

IMPROVED GRINDSTONE BOX, WITH A SLOW MOVEMENT ATTACHMENT FOR DRESSING OFF GRINDSTONES, No. 2½.

As it is well known that a grindstone cannot be properly dressed off when running at a high rate of speed, this appliance, which consists of a double set of cog wheels attached to our four foot box, can be thrown into gear in a moment, thereby reducing the rate of speed and enabling the grinder, with the use of a proper rest and our patent stone turning tool, to dress off the stone very quickly and perfectly, the wheels to be thrown out of gear when not needed.

MACHINISTS', (FOR POWER OR TREADLE, LIGHT WORK AND AMATEURS,) No. 3.

THIS is a very ornamental box, cast in one piece with legs bolted to the upper edge, and furnished with a rest, and splash boards to keep the drip off the floor.

They have a twelve inch pulley for power, and with or without a treadle for driving with the foot.

POWER GRINDSTONE, No. 4.

THESE are from three to six feet in diameter, hung
on round wrought iron shafts, from one and one-half,
to four inches thick, with self-adjusting plates and screws,
and running on heavy clamp boxes, bolted through the
sides of the frame, which are of yellow pine or oak, with
heavy oak legs securely bolted to the sides. The stone
is driven by a belt and pulley, which can be furnished of
any size.

HAND AND TREADLE GRINDSTONES, No. 5.

THESE are made of all sizes and grits, from twelve to thirty-six inches in diameter, and hung on strong wood frames, with self-adjusting cranks, and running on friction rollers or sockets. They are furnished with water-pot, handle and treadle, and are driven by hand, or can be turned with the foot without assistance. They are intended for farmers and mechanics generally, and cost less than to buy the stone and fixtures separately.

No. 6.   No. 7.

HIGH LEG GRINDSTONES.

THESE are from twelve to twenty-four inches in diameter, and of fine grit. They can be used when standing erect, and being driven by the foot with a treadle, they are a great convenience to amateurs, and are a good stone for family use.

No. 8.
SHIP GRINDSTONE, FOR GOVERNMENT SHIPS.

SHIP GRINDSTONE, FOR MERCHANT VESSELS,
No. 9.

THESE are from twelve to twenty-four inches in diame
ter. They are turned by hand, and are intended for ship's
use only, being made very low, so as to be used in a sitting
position on the deck of a vessel.

No. 10.

LORING & SONS' KITCHEN GRINDSTONE.

One of the most desirable things in a family is to have
sharp knives for the table, and the fixtures heretofore used
for the purpose have been so badly contrived as to be
almost useless. This article obviates these objections,
being durable, cheap, easily worked, and not liable to
get out of order. It is screwed to the kitchen table, and
by one turn of the handle, turns three and a half times,
which puts on a keen edge, without any danger of the
knife cutting the hand. When the stone is worn out, a
new one can be readily fitted for the spindle, so as to run
true without trouble. The stones vary from eight to
twelve inches in diameter.

FRANKLIN INSTITUTE EXHIBITION, OF 1874.

SILVER MEDAL AWARDED FOR

GRINDSTONE FIXTURES,

MADE AND DEPOSITED BY

J. HENRY MITCHELL,

602 Beach Street, Philadelphia.

FOR five sizes of iron boxes for machinists' use are made on a new plan, which combines lightness and cheapness with durability, the sides being strongly bolted together (instead of the whole being cast in one piece,) and the shaft is of wrought iron, with forged shoulders with Babbit metal boxes, and cast iron plates which hold the stone by friction on its sides by means of a screw and nut.

Two sizes of grindstone shafts made of the best quality of round iron from one inch to four inches in thickness, on which a heavy collar is forged and against which a thick cast-iron plate twelve to thirty inches in diameter rests; a screw is cut on the other end of the shaft on which a heavy nut is placed, which presses another cast-iron plate against the sides of the grindstone, leaving the centre free, and holding the stone perfectly firm by the pressure on its sides; this relieves the eye from the strain of the old fashioned square shaft and wedges, and prevents any possibility of the stone bursting when running, however fast.

HAND SHAFTS.

SOCKETS OR ROLLERS, CAST OR WROUGHT IRON.

THESE are made of various sizes, to suit stones from twelve to thirty-six inches in diameter, and of any thickness from two to six inches, with plates and screws, and both treadle and handle.

We have made great improvements in the manufacture of wrought iron shafts by the use of a right and left hand screw, which brings the stone in the centre of the frame, and as we make them in large quantities by the use of screw cutting machines, we can offer them at a small advance on the cost of cast iron shafts, which are so liable to break, especially in frosty weather.

SHIP STONE SHAFTS.

Rollers or sockets of cast iron, made similar to the others, but intended only for stones from twelve to eighteen inches in diameter.

FAMILY STONE FIXTURES.

(See Page 30.)

CAST IRON BOXES.

(See Pages 25, 26, Etc.,)

With clamp boxes, shaft and pulley, for three and four feet grindstones.

FRAMES.

Of all sizes, and made by machinery in the most substantial manner, of yellow pine or oak; well braced and bolted, with water boxes to catch the drip.

We also manufacture or keep for sale:

FRENCH BURR MILL STONES,
HULLING STONES,
BARLEY STONES,
COCALICO MILL STONES,
GRINDSTONE HACKERS.

3

MILL STONE PICKS.

Also: Stone Cutters' Grit, Pumice, and Scotch Hone.

GROCERS' SUGAR MILLS,

WITH GALVANIZED ROLLERS, TO PREVENT SOILING THE SUGAR.

ROLLERS.

No. 1.—4 x 8 inches.
No. 2.—4 x 10 inches.
No. 3.—5 x 12 inches.
No. 4.—5 x 15 inches.

(Extra strong for Steam Power.)

FRANKLIN INSTITUTE EXHIBITION, OF 1874

MEDAL AWARDED FOR

GRINDSTONES,

DEPOSITED BY

J. E. MITCHELL,

310 York Avenue, Philadelphia.

1st. The display of Grindstones comprises eight sorts or grits, from the finest to the coarsest, and are all turned off perfectly true with a patent tool, which does the work very rapidly. The uses they are put to, are :

1st. "Bay Chaleur," for Cutlery Grinding, and for Sharpening Fine Edge Tools.
2d. "New Castle," ⎫ for Saw and File Grinding, and for
3d. "Melling," ⎭ Sharpening Machinists' Tools.
4th. "Wickersly," for Grinding Saws.
5th. "Berea," for Edge Tools.
6th. "Massillon," for File Grinding.
7th. "Craigleith," for Edge Work, ⎫
8th. "Nova Scotia," for Fluting Work, ⎬ for Glass cutters.
  "New Castle," for Flat Work, ⎭

The "Craigleith" stones are only found in Scotland, and are of a peculiarly hard, yet sharp grit, and are the only kind of stone yet discovered, which will hold the edge necessary to cut glass.

These comprise but a small proportion of the various kinds of stones in use in the arts, there being a great variety of oil and whet stones for finishing the edges of tools; fine grit stones for polishing marble, &c.; curriers' rub stones, clearing stones and scouring stones, which are not exhibited for want of space.

36

POLISHING STONES, CURRIERS' STONES, CLEARING STONES AND SCOURING STONES.

FOR CURRIERS' USE.

CLEARING STONES.
Scotch, (Water of Ayr.)   Hindostan, (Orange.)   Welsh.

RUB STONES.
Huron, (very fine.)   Nova Scotia, (fine.)
New Castle, (coarse.)

SCOURING STONES.
Irish.   North River.   Slate.   Handles.

FIDDLING STONES.
Flat.   Round, (fine.)   Round, (coarse.)

POLISHING STONES.

SCOTCH HONE.
Rough, for Marble Polishers.   Squared.

MARBLE POLISHERS' GRIT.
Fine.   Coarse.

BLUE POLISHING STONE.
For Calico Printers.
Rough.   Sawed.

WATER OF AYR SLIPS.
For Metal Polishing.

PUMICE STONE.
GLASS SLICKERS.

OIL AND WHETSTONES.
Arkansas.   Washita.   Hindostan, (Orange.)
Novaculite.

SHOEMAKERS' RUBBERS.

HOLY STONES,
Of all sizes, (for ships' use.)

SCYTHE STONES.

Having visited the principal quarries in England, Ireland, Scotland and Wales, for the production of the various kinds of stones used by Curriers, Marble Polishers, Calico Printers and others, and having made arrangements for a full supply directly from the manufacturers, I am enabled to sell at the above low prices to the trade.

PORTLAND CEMENT.

FOR ROUGH CASTING, POINTING, &c.

IMPORTED DIRECT FROM THE FACTORY.

A pure Hydraulic Lime imported from England, where it is used extensively for pointing, rough casting, and ornamenting the fronts of buildings. It becomes as hard as stone by exposure to the weather, especially in damp places and under water, making a most excellent coating for cisterns, tanks, &c., and will even resist the action of the most powerful alkalies.

It is unsurpassed for pointing of stone rubble work, making the walls stronger, and effectually preventing rain or dampness from penetrating. This Cement mixed with a large proportion of sand is admirably adapted for cellar floors, and by mixing only ten per cent. of Cement with broken stone it forms " Beton," which would make an admirable foundation for roadways, becoming harder with age, instead of decaying like the wooden blocks. The best proportions have been found to be

FOR "BETON."

ONE PART OF CEMENT.
TEN PARTS BROKEN STONE.

FOR CELLARS.

ONE PART OF CEMENT.
FOUR PARTS OF SAND.

For POINTING, ROUGH CASTING, ETC., use one part Cement, and two parts of clean flint sand. One bushel of Cement and two of sand will cover four square yards, three-eighths of an inch thick.

☞PURE WHITE FLINT SAND, ROMAN, ROSENDALE AND LOUISVILLE, KY., CEMENTS.

PORTSILICA ARTIFICIAL STONE.

PLANT AND FOUNTAIN BASINS, BORDER EDGING, ORNAMENTAL TILES OF VARIOUS COLORS.

It can be moulded into any desired shape, and becomes as hard as a hard sandstone, but unlike sandstone it continues to harden especially when exposed to dampness. It is extensively used in Germany for ornamenting the fronts of houses and can be made of any desired color. The beautiful details of the imposing portals and in fact all parts of the Exposition Buildings, at Vienna, in 1873, were ornamented with this substance, which presented all the effects of elaborately carved stone work at infinitely less cost. It can also be made into highly ornamental tiles of beautiful colors, and which are very durable. Fountains or Plant basins, ten feet in diameter, which can be safely transported to a distance, and set up by an ordinary stonemason on a cheap brick or stone foundation, appearing as cut stone at a fraction of its cost. Several of these are now set up in the grounds of the Agricultural Department, at Washington, D. C. Flooring tiles of various colors and sizes, which are equal to stone or terra cotta at a less cost. It is believed that this substance will fill a necessity long felt in building operations for something which will be of an ornamental character, and of a soft neutral color, to take the place of red bricks and without being as costly as cut stone. It is firmly believed that Portsilica will meet all these requirements, and prove a valuable aid in the erection of ornamental and cheap buildings.

Send for price list to

WILSON MITCHELL, Manufacturer,
No. 310 YORK AVENUE.

Factory, Belmont and Girard Avenues, near Exposition Grounds, Philadelphia.

1776! CENTENNIAL DISPLAY! 1876

OF GRINDSTONES AND GRINDSTONE FIXTURES, IN MACHINERY HALL—CLASS 575, SECTION B 4, COLUMNS 28 AND 29.

Consisting of a handsome pedestal and column, formed of forty varieties of machinists' grindstones from all parts of the world, handsomely turned off with the patent turning tool, so as to represent the exact proportions of Tuscan column, 26 feet high.

MACHINISTS' GRINDSTONE AND FIXTURES.

Five sizes of grindstones in cast iron boxes, with rests and pulleys, finished and ready for use.

One double hung fixture, with two grindstones, (coarse and fine,) adjusted to keep perfectly true.

Five sizes of grindstones in wood frames, ready for use.

Twenty grindstones from 1000 to 4000 pounds each, of various grits, and turned perfectly true. Oil Stones, Lathe Stones, &c., &c.